USING THIS BOOK

*Children learn to read by **reading**, but they need help to begin with.*

When you have read the story on the left-hand pages aloud to the child, go back to the beginning of the book and look at the pictures together.

Encourage children to read the sentences under the pictures. If they don't know a word, give them a chance to 'guess' what it is from the illustrations, before telling them.

There are more suggestions for helping children to learn to read in the *Parent/Teacher* booklet.

British Library Cataloguing in Publication Data
McCullagh, Sheila K.
    Three wishes and one more. — (Puddle Lane; stage 3/6).
    1. Readers — 1950-
    I. Title   II. Rowe, Gavin   III. Series
    428.6   PE1119
    ISBN 0-7214-0961-X

First edition

Published by Ladybird Books Ltd Loughborough Leicestershire UK
Ladybird Books Inc Lewiston Maine 04240 USA

© Text and layout SHEILA McCULLAGH MCMLXXXVII
© In publication LADYBIRD BOOKS LTD MCMLXXXVII

Printed in England

Three wishes and one more

written by SHEILA McCULLAGH
illustrated by GAVIN ROWE

This book belongs to:

Ladybird Books

Jennifer Jane
lived in Puddle Lane.
She lived with her grandmother
in a little house,
halfway down the lane.
(Jennifer's grandmother
always called her 'Jenny'.)

Jennifer Jane
lived in Puddle Lane.
She lived with her grandmother.

Jennifer Jane had a magic wishing penny.
If she held the magic penny
in her hand, and wished,
the wish came true.
Jennifer Jane kept the magic penny
in an old china shoe,
on the shelf over the fireplace.
"A china shoe is the safest place
for a magic penny,"
said Grandmother.

Jennifer Jane had
a magic penny.
Grandmother put it
in a china shoe.

One winter's evening,
Grandmother was going out.
"I shall be home late, Jenny,"
said Grandmother.
"Have supper on the table,
when I come back."
"I will," said Jennifer Jane.
"If you use the magic penny,
remember this," said Grandmother.
"You must **never** wish more
than three times, in any one day.
If you do, the penny will vanish away."
"I will remember, Grandmother,"
said Jennifer Jane.
"I won't forget."

Grandmother said,
''Have supper on the table
when I come back.''

Grandmother went out.

Jennifer Jane put on an apron,

and tidied up the house.

Then she began to lay the table

all ready for supper.

The grandfather clock struck

six o'clock,

but Grandmother had not come home.

Jennifer Jane
put on her apron.
The grandfather clock
struck six o'clock.

Jennifer Jane began to feel lonely.
She went to the window,
and pulled back the curtains.
It was very dark in Puddle Lane.
There was no one about at all.

Jennifer Jane
went to the window.
She looked out into Puddle Lane.
It was very dark in Puddle Lane.

The grandfather clock struck
seven o'clock, and still
Grandmother had not come home.
"I must do something,"
said Jennifer Jane.
She went to the fireplace,
and climbed on a stool.
She took down the china shoe.
She took out the silver penny,
and held it in her hand.
She went to the window, and
looked out into Puddle Lane.
It was very dark.
"I wish there were lanterns
in Puddle Lane,"
said Jennifer Jane.

The grandfather clock
struck seven o'clock.
Jennifer Jane got the china shoe.
She took out the magic penny.
''I wish there were lanterns
in Puddle Lane,'' she said.

The next moment, beautiful coloured
lanterns were hanging outside the houses
in Puddle Lane.
Some of them were blue,
and some of them were green.
Some of them were yellow,
and some of them were red.
"It's lovely! It's lovely!"
cried Jennifer Jane.
"Now Grandmother can see the way,
when she comes home in the dark."

There were beautiful lanterns
in Puddle Lane.
Some lanterns were blue.
Some lanterns were green.
Some lanterns were yellow.
Some lanterns were red.

Jennifer Jane stood at the window,
looking out into Puddle Lane.
The grandfather clock struck eight o'clock,
and still Grandmother had not come home.
It was very bright in Puddle Lane,
but it was very quiet.
"I know!" cried Jennifer Jane.
"I know what I'll do!"
She held the magic penny in her hand.
"I wish for some music,"
said Jennifer Jane.
"I wish there was music,
in Puddle Lane."

The grandfather clock
struck eight o'clock.
Jennifer Jane said,
''I wish there was music
in Puddle Lane.''

The very next moment,
there was a man in Puddle Lane.
He was playing the violin.
He was rather a strange looking man.
He was dressed in silver and red.
But he was playing such a dancing tune,
that Jennifer Jane began to dance.
She dropped the magic penny
into the pocket in her apron.
She opened the door,
and danced out into Puddle Lane.

Jennifer Jane danced.
She opened the door, and
danced out into Puddle Lane.

The doors of the other houses opened,
and all the people in Puddle Lane
came out of their houses to dance.
Sarah and Davy were there, and
so were Hari and Gita.
Even old Mr Gotobed woke up,
and came out in his nightcap
to join in the dance.

All the people in Puddle Lane
came out of their houses to dance.

Jennifer Jane looked down at her dress.
She was still wearing her apron!
"I mustn't dance in an apron,"
said Jennifer Jane.
She took the magic penny
out of her pocket,
and held it in her hand.
"I wish to be dressed in a beautiful dress,
the most beautiful dress in Candletown,"
said Jennifer Jane.

Jennifer Jane had her apron on.
"I wish for a beautiful dress,"
she said.

And the very next moment, Jennifer Jane
was dressed in a beautiful dress.
She went dancing up and down the lane,
and everyone stopped to look at her.

Jennifer Jane had a beautiful dress.
She danced up and down the lane.

She had nearly danced
to the top of the lane
when she saw her grandmother.
Grandmother had just come
into the lane at the other end.
Jennifer Jane suddenly remembered
that she had promised
to have supper all ready,
when Grandmother came home.

Jennifer Jane saw Grandmother
come into the lane.

Jennifer Jane put her hand in her pocket,
and took out the magic penny.
"I wish for supper," she said.
"Supper must be ready on the table,
before Grandmother gets home."
But that was the fourth wish!
Jennifer Jane had had three wishes already.

"I wish for supper,"
said Jennifer Jane.
"Supper must be on the table."

The very next moment, the lane was dark.
The lanterns were gone.
The music was gone.
All the people went back
into their houses.
The lane was silent.
Jennifer Jane and her grandmother
were alone in the lane.
Jennifer felt for the magic penny,
but the magic penny had gone.
So had her beautiful dress.
She was dressed in her apron again.

The lanterns were gone.
The music was gone.
All the people
went back into the houses.

Jennifer Jane ran to her grandmother.
"Oh, Grandmother, Grandmother,
look what I've done!"
cried Jennifer Jane.
"I wished four times in one day,
and the magic penny has gone!
I've lost the magic wishing penny!"
The tears ran down her face.

Jennifer Jane
ran to her grandmother.
She began to cry.

Grandmother put her arms
around Jennifer Jane.
"Don't cry, Jenny," she said. "Don't cry.
We were very happy, before you found
the magic wishing penny.
We don't need a magic penny.
We can live very well without it.
And you never know what may happen.
You may find the penny again.
Don't cry, Jenny. Come along in.
I've brought a cherry pie
home with me.
We'll have that for supper."

"Don't cry, Jenny. Don't cry,"
said Grandmother.

So Jennifer Jane and her grandmother
both went into the house.
The fire was burning in the grate,
and the table was laid for supper.
Grandmother put the cherry pie
on the table.
Jennifer Jane dried her tears,
and they both sat down to supper.

Jennifer Jane
and her grandmother
sat down to supper.

Parent/teacher please note:

Learning to anticipate what comes next is part of learning to read.
Look at the picture on page 41, and read the words at the top of the page. Then ask: "What happened next?"

Turn over to page 42, to see what happened next.

One day, when Jennifer Jane
had the magic wishing penny
she held the penny in her hand,
and wished.
She wished for someone to play with.

There was a knock at the door.
What do you think happened next?

Now read this page and follow the instructions.

One day, Jennifer Jane
wished for a chocolate cake.

Take a piece of paper, and draw for yourself
what happened next.

Have you read these stories about the people in Puddle Lane?

Stage 3

from Old Mr Gotobed

from The magic penny